You Are Too Beautiful

(New Age Poetry About Love; Ideas for those Left on Earth)

Youssef Khalim

ISBN: 978-0-9787810-9-5
ISBN-13: 978-0978781095

DEDICATION

To: Larisa Khalim (the real or ideal soul-mate: inspiration)

       Tonya Tracy Khalim and
Runako Soyini Khalim, (my most beloved daughters)

       Mother and Grandmother and Great-grandmother, (my most beloved maternal biological ancestors, and spiritual antecedents)

       M. A. Garvey (one of my 7 M's: my role models)

       Youssef Khalim II; III (my most beloved sons)

       Father and Grandfather and Great-grandfather, (my

       most beloved paternal biological ancestors, and spiritual antecedents).

To: The Forerunners and Reincarnation sources (beloved biological ancestors and spiritual antecedents), and The Almighty (our Spiritual Father), from whence we come.

CONTENTS

ACKNOWLEDGMENTS

To: The Forerunners and Reincarnation sources (beloved
        biological ancestors and spiritual antecedents), and
        The Almighty (our Spiritual Father), from whence we
        come.

        The Art Piece used with "In Love In Kiss," p. 3, is from
        "The Realms Of Magic: Boris Vallejo Image Gallery,
        Vallejo bin/ BV02.gif, located at
        http://users.aol.com/varian/boris-links.html.

1 YOU ARE TOO BEAUTIFUL

You are
Too beautiful:

Your eyes focus the loveliness of all creation.

Your smile makes everything stand still and watch you (in a state of awe).

And you are radiant, glowing: Beautiful.

The beauty of your mouth invites a million kisses.

You are magnetic, intelligent, gorgeous, sexy;

Expressive
Music flows each time you speak.

Too bad some folks may never know you
Because one cannot say
Too many times that

You are
Too beautiful.

2 YOU ARE NOT SIMPLY A 10

You are not simply
A 10.

For, you are
Wonderful
Magnificent
Incomparable.

You are Woman
Goddess,
Queen:
What "woman" means.

Numbers cannot measure
Eyes that glorify our Maker.

Men invented veils to shield them from the awesome feelings your
Smile generates.
And they invented kisses just to taste your mouth.

Then, God instilled the
7 virtues in your heart.

For, you are

Incomparable
Magnificent
Wonderful.

You are not simply
A 10.

3 IN LOVE, IN KISS

We make the brightest
Love-light in the
Galaxies of love:
I taste
The gateway to your soul,
Inhale
Your closeness, softness;
Drink
Your sweetness, warmness.

I soak
Myself in you,
In love, in kiss:
& GLOW.
We make the BRIGHTEST
Love-light in the
Galaxies, in love.

4 FOREVER WITH YOU

With you,
I want to:

Live, forever
Be happy, eternally
Turn the world; unlock its diary
Harness light; announce utopia
Befriend the poor; converse with time
Transact with God; & love completely
Inherit the earth, & bless the stars
Know good from evil; & end injustice
Tame The Word; rest, in myself

&

Live forever,
With you.

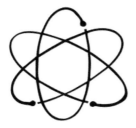

5 ADORATIONS

The spark of God in me
Adores you
And

I love you,
Bless you

In my heart where
You are light.

You lift and warm my sacred soul if I just
Think of you.

You turn me on beyond all earthly bounds,
And send me floating through this Milky Way.

Just as sure as sparks of God return to Him,
The spark of you does

Fan me to a flaming fire,
And

Adorations of you
Never
Ever
Cease.

6 A FORCE FOR GOOD

You radiate life-giving force:

I feel the rays of heaven in your presence.

Joy is sprung when you come near
And here is changed to gladness.

Your force unleashes wells of kindness
And I am mindful God is Beauty, Love, and Grace.

The smile you give has legendary might,
And I might add, I'm left in midair...
Groping for air (slightly overwhelmed).

Your force creates spring heat
These record-setting, coldest days of February:
Winter is a breeze.

I seek your favor, everlasting bonding.
And may that Mighty Force of Heaven
Bless you
(As you have my life).

7 LORRAINE

When soil is dry, Loe'rain!
Rain on the earth L' rain.
Come by and by,
Oh wondrous drop,
I say a sigh, reach for the sky
Before I die, Lorraine.

Me Injun dance for rain:
Peal thunderbolt
Whiplash a lightning flash
& kick a mountain 'part
Unzip the sky
Shake down the stars,
Straw 'way the seas,
Unearth the Pyrenees;
Ring laughter from a rhino,
Sing a lullaby for rain.

I'll walk the mist
Remand a serpent's hiss.
End by-and-by
And cage a lie;
Make dumb men talk,
Curtail the leopard's stalk;
Make eagles chirp,

Rework the earth;
Drive crazies sane,
Write me a better name, for rain.

I'll ordain kings,
Stop man from being mean,
Bring in thy kingdom come,
Decree the end of night,
Allow just justice, light, and right.
And like my father would rather,
Bring all the world together.

When earth'n heaven meet
Torrential rains come down
Because I swim the rain,
Glide gently o'er rain.
I whet the rain.
I even wet the rain:

'Til God, you, I
Are One-&-the-same!
I've got to have-L'rain.

8 LOVE AT WORK

Just as sure as mammals mate,
When I see or think of you,
I love you.

Your body draws me with the force
That holds the worlds in orbit.

My body absolutely wants to love you.

For, "atoms" fuse to show the force of
Love at work.

Day by day
I love you more & more.

For, just as sure as mammals mate,
My heart just loves you
When I see or think of you.

Just as sure as "atoms" fuse to show the force of
Love at work,
My heart says yes to you a trillion times.

And just as sure as God exists,
My love for you will always be in force.

For, mammals mate to show the force of
Love at work.

9 YOU MAKE MY ENGINE ROAR

You make my engine roar
With all its might:

You make it soar

& take to flight.

My engine used to waver and sputter.
It was like a ship without a rudder.

I used to say, " You gotta use all your cylinders"
But, my engine kept giving me the finger.

You really get my motor going;
I need your octane every morning.

I long to see you every night
To keep my motor roaring right.

With all my might,
I love your octane,

And long to soar with you
(A morning, noon, or night time)
On flights to anywhere
To make our engines roar.

10 HOUSE OF PLEASURE

I desire to show you the greatest joys of

Pleasure
Adventure, and
Contentment

In the Everlasting House of Love
Because I love you.

Come for adventure whenever you need it,
And I will give the joy you never want to end.

I know just where to push your buttons for contentment;
My pleasure is to
Give you Pleasure
Since I love you.

I will show you:
All doors are made of trust and patience
Unity and harmony will overlook the windows
The beds are made of warmth & celebration
The sun and moon will light the rooms
The House sits on the wheels of time
Peace and excitement grow like potted plants
You provide the beauty
And you can choose to grow in grace & love.

We will build it on the building blocks of love
Because, only in love do we build the Everlasting House of

Pleasure
Adventure, and
Contentment,

And show you
I love you.

11 MEMO

Date: **Valentine's Day**

Subject: **Our Mission, Methods, and Motto**

From: **Me and US**

To: **The Team**

Application: **Application is for today, tomorrow, or any day**

To give your best is better than to give.

It is our pleasure to give total customer satisfaction.

Your teamwork & cooperation (always)
Makes it better;

So, thanks for your contribution
Because

You make the difference!

Now & ever,
Let us succeed together.

HAPPY VALENTINES!!!

12 SLICES

I think of you
As my wonderful
Golden,
Slice of God:

To please,
To hold
In my arms,
And to talk with;
& to love,

And to make
More slices
With.

13 CREATION AND MULTIPLICATION

When I'm with you, or when I think of you
I become the perfect love organ, for you:
To love you
Touch you, tease you, caress you, hold you in my mouth;
To fill you; free you, build you: bind you,
Shield you, assist you, (in rapture, bliss), to please you.

When I'm with you, or when I think of you
I become the shape/form, design & mind (to be used by you)-
A tool, a purpose (for you to use):
To clear a path, & place for you; to build for you.
I become created (by you, for us),
Which makes one; & with Him, makes three;
Which becomes One perfect love organ,
Which creates, in the service of millions.

14 MAGIC EYES

When you look up, I'm still amazed to see the color green:
The color spring, the color of your eyes
Excite and churn me, (revving-up my springtime might).
The color's healing (your green is so appealing),
I love your lovely eyes.

And looks into your eyes
Keep me in springtime heat (throughout the year).
I long to taste you, take you
Rub it on, & rub it in.
So heal me with your eyes.

Your eyes turn hazel, brown sometimes,
Bring me to earth and warm my heart.
I tend to melt, before excitement builds.
I delve into the caring brown
(Your lashes shutter; so do I).
Entice & thrill me, warm & chill me
Fix me up; come, drug me with your eyes.

Beside that lake,
Your eyes turn grey and look blue,
Leave me awash, and breathless;
Lift me to the stars, boundless.
I see forever, groundless,
That partly sunny day.

Your eyes peel off the space between two.
You smile & sow the seed, "I love you."
(Give me that magic potion, balm & cure)
Caress my soul, undress my heart;
I'll take your smiling eyes.

With more exploratory time,
Let's find a laboratory life:

And meet & greet more
often (keeping to
appointment)
To give amazing love & healing,
And share the magic, eyes.

15 STATUESQUE

My blood warms in your presence.
My mind rewinds, I reminisce about you.

Your elegance prolongs this summer,
No wonder, I'm in love with autumn
Thinking 'bout you.

You're a lovely word called statuesque,
I've got to have you so my soul can rest.

You give a smile and I heat up.
When I watch you walk I can't get enough.

This sudden day, life has a lift,
It's wild, just contemplating if's
About you.

You're a lovely word called statuesque,
I've got to have you so my soul can rest.

16 MY THOUGHTS ABOUT YOU NEVER GO AWAY

I just thought I'd take this time to say
That my thoughts about you never go away:

I thought about you when I could
I thought about you when I should-
Not be thinking about anything but what
I was supposed to be about.

I thought about you daytime, night time
& in the tiny spaces in between time.
I thought about you in real time, suspended time, borrowed
time, space time, and when it was time out.

I thought I was thinking about you once
When the thought escaped me
(& to this day I'm not really sure about what about you
I was thinking about).

I thought about you one day when I think
Time stood still, and yet, I was still thinking about you
(Now think about that).

I rode up and down a street with your name
(just think), that street will never be the same.

Once, I was thinking about how much I love you when I
Actually consumed you;
And that was the end of that.

I thought about you one day
When it was really many days later.
So, I think-maybe, time just leaped ahead
(& it was not leap year that year).

I thought about you while alone in my car
And you were parked in my mind in a crowded bar.

I thought about you lovingly, tenderly,
Roughly, and gingerly:
I can't think of an end to you & me.

I thought about you at night & you woke me up.
And on a bright sunny day I'm entranced by your love.

I thought to show how much I care,
I thought to bless you in all my prayers.

I thought of a place for you this winter time
That put you in a place somewhere in summer time.

I put an easy, warm breeze in the air
That gently toyed with & tossed your hair.
Now do I care- or what?

I thought about you long & I thought about you hard,
I thought 'til the end wrapped around to the start.

I just thought I'd take this time to say
That my thoughts about you never go away.

17 TAILOR MADE

Come, let me wrap you
Like the dress you're wearing.

And if you care,
Caress
The way it clings to you.

Come, let me clothe you
With a passion flame that's everlasting;
Groove together:

Let's dance forever,
And play
In love that's tailor made.

Let us uncover love together
& share the reason
That our lives have crossed,

Design sensations that will
Blanket God's Creation

Cast off all doubt that only love is real.
And groove together

Dance forever,
And play
In love that's tailor made.

18 I VOW TO LOVE EACH DIMPLE EQUALLY

I vow to love each dimple equally
Each time you smile

And taste your mouth
Through words you speak

To touch your form
In passing glances

See your eyes
As seen in heaven

Love you through and through
Your presence

Love you with
All earthy passion.

I vow to love each dimple equally
And to double goodness to you

And begin the beyond,
Measure time in endless pleasure.

I vow to love each dimple equally
And to love you twice as good

Since you have two equally good
Reasons to smile.

19 I LOVE YOU ALL OVER AGAIN

Every time I see you,
I fall in love all over again.

I do it over & over & over & over
& over & over again.

I like to do it all over again.
I'd like to love you all over
Again.

And if I ever meet someone new,
I'll pretend that it is you
And love you all over again.
I want to love you all over Again.

I have to love you all over
Again.

Every time I see you,
You thrill me over & over again,
I love you over & over again.

I want you
Over & over again.

Come back & thrill me all over again,

So I can love you all over again.

I have to love you all over
Again.

22

20 ABOUT THE AUTHOR, AND OTHER BOOKS

Youssef Khalim obtained Unity in yoga on about 7/20/80. He says, "we will recombine into one faith, Judaism, Christianity, and Islam." He has been able to "see" and experience some amazing information about USA presidents Jefferson, Lincoln, and Obama; and also Prophets Moses, Muhammad, and Solomon - in visions, lucid dreams, and in meditation. Khalim makes reincarnation (resurrection) central again in our western religions. He resides in the Chicagoland area. And he is the father of Tonya, Runako, and Noah. His websites include: http://amazon.com http://lulu.com and http://sunracommunications.com

OTHER BOOKS

Youssef Khalim's books include *People Of The Future/ Day; I Love You Back; The Resurrection of Noah: You Look So Good; Healing Begins With The Mind; Jubilee Worldwide; Lara, Forever; Tanisha Love; Galina, All About Love; I Call My Sugar, Candie; Natalia, With Love; Svetlana, Angel Of Love; Lori, My Dream Girl*; *Love of My Life*; and *The Second Coming!*

CPSIA information can be obtained
at www.ICGtesting.com
Printed in the USA
LVIC06n1742081013
356007LV00012B

9 780978 781095